Family Reading Time

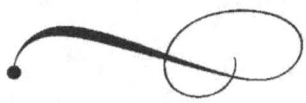

A Grandfather's Dinner Table Recitations

Dr. Ernest Cronin

Copyright © 2022 by Ernest Cronin

All rights reserved. No part of this publication may be reproduced or transmitted in any form or by any means, electronic or mechanical, including photocopying and recording, or by any information storage and retrieval system, except in the case of brief quotations for use in articles and reviews, without written permission from the author.

The views expressed in this book are the author's and do not necessarily reflect those of the publisher.

7710-T Cherry Park Dr, Ste 224
Houston, TX 77095
(713) 766-4271

Cover design: www.HarvestCreek.net

ISBN: 978-1-64830-423-1

Dedication

I dedicate this book to my parents,
Edward C. Cronin, and Elaine Dattner Cronin

Contents

Introduction	XI
Blessings	1
Portia's Speech	2
A Red, Red Rose	3
Stopping By Woods On A Snowy Evening	4
In Flanders Fields	5
Lovely Lady Dressed In Blue	6
Miniver Cheevy	7
Heart Of Darkness	9
Tyger Tyger	10
Song Of The Witches	11
The Road Not Taken	12
Immortality	13
Jaques' Monologue	14
It Was The Best Of Times	15
It Is A Far, Far Better Thing	15
Dreams	16
16 Tons	17
Sonnet 18: Shall I Compare Thee To A Summer's Day?	18
Sonnet 19: When I Consider How My Light Is Spent	19
Daffodils	20
Fog	21
O Danny Boy	22
To Thine Own Self Be True	23
How Sharper	24
Cowards	25
Barbara Frietchie	26

My Feet Are Wearied	29
Juliet's Speech	30
My Kingdom For A Horse!	31
Teddy Roosevelt One-Liners #1	32
Death, Be Not Proud	33
To Sleep	34
Mark Antony's Speech	35
To A Mouse On Turning Her Up In Her Nest With The Plough	37
Teddy Roosevelt One-Liners #2	39
The Lamb	40
Man In The Arena	41
Shakespeare One-Liners #1	42
Father Malloy	43
God Bless America	44
Meditation 17	45
The Hill	47
Teddy Roosevelt One-Liners #3	49
Charge Of The Light Brigade	50
Lucinda Matlock	52
Pledge Of Allegiance	53
Teddy Roosevelt One-Liners #4	54
Trees	55
O Captain! My Captain	56
To A Louse, On Seeing One On A Lady's Bonnet At Church	57
St. Crispian's Day Speech	59
Casey At The Bat	61
In The Land Where We Were Dreaming	63
Prayer, And Hope Of Victory	67
A Land Without Ruins	68
Hark To The Shouting Wind!	69

A Song Of Eternity In Time	70
Fire And Ice	71
Richard Cory	72
Tomorrow, And Tomorrow, And Tomorrow	73
Niccol Machiavelli One-Liners	74
To The Virgins, To Make Much Of Time	75
When You Are Old	76
Sonnet 116	77
I Carry Your Heart With Me	78
Judged By The Company One Keeps	79
When I Too Long	80
The Swing	81
Who Has Seen The Wind?	82
My Shadow	83
The Owl And The Pussy-Cat	84
The Road Ahead	86
Ronald Reagan One-Liners #1	87
Ronald Reagan One-Liners #2	88
The Windhover	89
Ronald Reagan One-Liners #3	90
Riddle Of The World	91
The Star-Spangled Banner	92
Ronald Reagan One-Liners #4	93
Weather	94
Sarah Cynthia Sylvia Stout	97
Little Edgar Smith	99
The Destruction Of Sennacherib	100
If—	101
Marcus Aurelius One-Liners	103
Mother Teresa #1	104

Mother Teresa #2	105
Mother Teresa #3	106
Mother Teresa #4	107
The Lord Is My Shepherd	108
The Words Of The Preacher	109
About Dr. Cronin	110

Preface

My wife and I raised eight children. We made a significant effort to have frequent evening meals together. These dinners helped us to stay connected with our children and their activities and interests.

Central aspects of our evening repast were first the formal blessing, (this is the first item in the anthology) the second aspect was a recitation of a poem or prose passage and the discussion which followed. This was almost always enjoyable and educational. My wife Candy is a primary reason we had the dinner time recitations in the first place. She also encouraged me to compile this anthology.

I decided to compile this anthology to give families appropriate, convenient material they might use with their family meals. Of course, individuals may enjoy reading this anthology anytime.

I do not know what effect this ultimately had on our children's character or behavior. My wife Candy had a dominant role in their Christian formation, but even today they still sometimes refer to us as "the parental unit." We did try to stick together when dealing with discipline or most important matters vis a vis our admirable progeny.

We are both proud that all eight of our children remain faithful Catholic Christians in this chaotic world. Perhaps our evening recitations and discussions did play a role. Our grown children appreciate the sanctity of life and welcome the next generation of children into family life. They are forming their own children for a kind, faithful, generous, holy, productive life with salvation as the ultimate goal. I hope you enjoy these reflections of our heritage.

I want to thank my children and grandchildren for their suggestions and support:

Erin and Oscar De La Cruz, their children, Julia, Mark, and Maria

Christopher and Andrea Cronin, their children, Moire, Aonghus, Judith, Evelyn, and Killian.

Eileen and Thomas Hubbard.

Mollie and Karl Ullrich, their children, Michael, Christopher, Peter, Helen, Anna, George, Henry, and Genevieve.

Brendan and Clair Cronin, their children, Aiden, Isabelle, Blaise, Sebastian, and Evangeline.

Carol and Dave Kelly, their children, C. J., and Lucy.

Sean and Margaret Cronin, their children, Jude, Felicity, Olive, and Basil.

Sheila and Andrew Santos, and their children, Caleb, John, and Sofia.

Finally, I want to thank Karl Ullrich, my son-in-law, for editing and formatting.

Introduction

This anthology is a particular slice of English and American literature that I find entertaining, fascinating, and educational. It is a small anthology collected from my personal preferences. Many selections are from authors I like who have stood the test of time, such as William Shakespeare, John Milton, William Blake, Robert Burns, Robert Frost, etc.

Many common topics are treated in manifold ways by various poets. For example, the prevalent topic of romantic love is presented in varying modes. There is Robert Burns glorious and intimate, "A Red, Red Rose," Shakespeare's, "Shall I Compare thee to a Summers Day," is staider, while Robert Herrick's "To the Virgins, to Make Much of Time," is much more sanguine.

There are inspirational readings, such as John Donne's masterpiece the 17th Meditation, (This Bell Tolling Softly for Another Says to Me, Thou Must Die). Educational poems like Robert Burn's "To a Mouse" and "To a Louse" give us the famous lines, "The best-laid schemes of mice and men often go astray," and "oh would some power the gift to give us, to see ourselves as others see us."

Inspirational, poignant, and meaningful quotes by several renowned individuals from Marcus Aurelius to Mother Teresa, such as "the happiness of your life depends upon the quality of your thoughts," and "kind words can be short and easy to speak, but their echoes are truly endless" are presented.

I have included as a sort of cameo appearance, two amateur poems I wrote. I thought they might feel good surrounded by such famous poems.

This anthology is inspired by the family dinner recitations my wife and I had with our eight children as they were growing up. I hope it might be useful to other families or individuals who love good literature.

Blessings

Bless us, O Lord and these Thy gifts,
which we are about to receive through Thy bounty,
through Christ, our Lord. Amen.

Mary Queen of peace: may the souls of the faithfully
departed, through the mercy of God
Rest in peace. Amen.

Praise be to the Incarnate Word now, and forever. Amen.

Portia's Speech
(The Merchant of Venice)

The quality of mercy is not strain'd,
It droppeth as the gentle rain from heaven
Upon the place beneath: it is twice blest;
It blesseth him that gives and him that takes:
'Tis mightiest in the mightiest: it becomes
The throned monarch better than his crown;
His sceptre shows the force of temporal power,
The attribute to awe and majesty,
Wherein doth sit the dread and fear of kings;
But mercy is above this sceptred sway;
It is enthroned in the hearts of kings,
It is an attribute to God himself;
And earthly power doth then show likest God's
When mercy seasons justice.

William Shakespeare

A Red, Red Rose

O my love is like a red, red rose
That's newly sprung in June
O my love is like the melody
That's sweetly played in tune.

So fair art thou, my bonnie lass,
So deep in love am I;
And I will love thee still, my dear
Till all the seas gang dry.

Till all the seas gang dry, my dear,
And the rocks melt with the sun;
I will love thee still, my dear,
While the sands of life shall run.

And fare thee well, my only love
And fare thee well a while!
And I will come again, my love,
Though it were ten thousand miles.

Robert Burns

Stopping by Woods on a Snowy Evening

Whose woods these are I think I know.
His house is in the village though;
He will not see me stopping here
To watch his woods, fill up with snow.

My little horse must think it queer
To stop without a farmhouse near
Between the woods and frozen lake
The darkest evening of the year.

He gives his harness bells a shake
To ask if there is some mistake.
The only other sound's the sweep
Of easy wind and downy flake.

The woods are lovely, dark, and deep,
But I have promises to keep,
And miles to go before I sleep,
And miles to go before I sleep.

Robert Frost

In Flanders Fields

In Flanders fields the poppies blow
Between the crosses, row on row
That mark our place; and in the sky
The larks, still bravely singing, fly
Scarce heard amid the guns below.

We are the Dead. Short days ago
We lived, felt dawn, saw sunset glow,
Loved and were loved, and now we lie,
In Flanders fields.

Take up our quarrel with the foe:
To you from failing hands we throw
The torch; be yours to hold it high.
If ye break faith with us who die
We shall not sleep, though poppies grow
In Flanders fields.

John McCrae

Lovely Lady Dressed in Blue

Lovely Lady dressed in blue—
Teach me how to pray!
God was just your little boy,
Tell me what to say!

Did you lift Him up, sometimes,
Gently on your knee?
Did you sing to Him the way
Mother does to me?

Did you hold His hand at night?
Did you ever try
Telling stories of the world?
O! And did He cry?

Do you really think He cares
If I tell Him things—
Little things that happen? And
Do the Angels' wings

Make a noise? And can He hear
Me if I speak low?
Does He understand me now?
Tell me—for you know.

Lovely Lady dressed in blue—
Teach me how to pray!
God was just your little boy,
And you know the way.

Mary Dixon Thayer

Miniver Cheevy

Miniver Cheevy, child of scorn,
Grew lean while he assailed the seasons;
He wept that he was ever born,
And he had reasons.

Miniver loved the days of old
When swords were bright, and steeds were prancing;
The vision of a warrior bold
Would set him dancing.

Miniver sighed for what was not,
And dreamed, and rested from his labors;
He dreamed of Thebes and Camelot,
And Priam's neighbors.

Miniver mourned the ripe renown
That made so many a name so fragrant;
He mourned Romance, now on the town,
And Art a vagrant.

Miniver loved the Medici,
Albeit he'd never seen one;
He would have sinned incessantly
Could he have been one.

Miniver cursed the commonplace
And eyed a khaki suit with loathing;
He missed the medieval grace
Of iron clothing.

Miniver scorned at the gold he sought,
But sore annoyed was he without it;

Miniver thought, and thought, and thought,
And thought about it.

Miniver Cheevy, born too late,
Scratched his head and kept on thinking;
Miniver coughed, and called it fate,
And kept on drinking.

Edwin Arlington Robinson

Heart of Darkness

"And perhaps in this is the whole difference;
perhaps all the wisdom, and all truth, and all sincerity,
are just compressed into that inappreciable moment
of time in which we step over the threshold of the invisible."

Joseph Conrad

Tyger Tyger

Tyger Tyger, burning bright,
In the forests of the night;
What immortal hand or eye,
Could frame thy fearful symmetry?

In what distant deeps or skies,
Burnt the fire of thine eyes?
On what wings dare he aspire?
What the hand, dare seize the fire?

And what shoulder, and what art,
Could twist the sinews of thy heart?
And when thy heart began to beat,
What dread hand? And what dread feet?

What the hammer? What the chain,
In what furnace was thy brain?
What the anvil? What dread grasp,
Dare its deadly terrors clasp!

When the stars threw down their spears
And water'd heaven with their tears:
Did he smile his work to see?
Did he who made the Lamb make thee?

William Blake "Songs of Experience"

Song of the Witches

Fillet of a Finney snake,
In the cauldron boil and bake;
Eye of newt and toe of frog,
Wool of bat and tongue of dog,
Adder's fork and blind-worm's sting
Lizard's leg and owlet's wing,
For a charm of powerful trouble,
Like a hell-broth boil and bubble.

Double, double, toil and trouble;
fire burn and cauldron bubble.
Cool it with a baboon's blood,
Then the charm is firm and good.

William Shakespeare (Macbeth)

The Road Not Taken

Two roads diverged in a yellow wood,
And sorry I could not travel both
And be one traveler, long I stood
And looked down one as far as I could
To where it bent in the undergrowth;

Then took the other, just as fair,
And having perhaps the better claim,
Because it was grassy and wanted wear;
Though as for that the passing there
Had worn them really about the same,

And both that morning equally lay
In leaves no step had trodden back.
Oh, I kept the first for another day!
Yet knowing how way leads on to way,
I doubted if I should ever come back.

I shall be telling this with a sigh
Somewhere ages and ages hence:
Two roads diverged in a wood, and I—
I took the one less traveled by,
And that has made all the difference.

Robert Frost

Immortality

Do not stand at my grave and weep,
I am not there. I do not sleep.

I am a thousand winds that blow,
I am the diamond glints on snow,
I am the sunlight on ripened grain,
I am the gentle autumn rain.

When you awaken in the morning's hush
I am the swift uplifting rush
Of quiet birds encircled flight.

I am the soft stars that shine at night.
Do not stand at my grave and cry,
I am not there. I did not die.

Mary Elizabeth Frye

Jaques' Monologue

All the world's a stage,
And all men and women merely players;
They have their exits and their entrances;
And one man in his time plays many parts,
His acts begin seven stages.
At first the infant,
Mewling and puking in the nurse's arms;
And then the whiny school-boy with his satchel
And shining morning face, creeping like snail
Unwilling to school.
And then the lover, sighing like a furnace....
Then a soldier jealous in honor....
And then the justice....
Full of wise saws and modern instances....
And so he plays his part....
Last scene of all,
That ends this strange eventful history,
Is second childlessness and mere oblivion;
Sans teeth, sans eyes, sans taste, stands everything.

William Shakesspeare, "As You like It"

It was The Best of Times

"It was the best of times, it was the worst of times,
it was the age of wisdom, it was the age of foolishness,
it was the epoch of belief, it was the epoch of incredulity,
it was the season of light, it was the season of darkness,
it was the spring of hope, it was the winter of despair."

It Is a Far, Far Better Thing

"It is a far, far better thing that I do, than I have ever
done; it is a far, far better rest that I go to
than I have ever known."

Charles Dickens, "A Tale of Two Cities"

Dreams

Hold fast to dreams
For if dreams die
Life is a broken-winged bird
That cannot fly.

Hold fast to dreams
For when dreams go
Life is a barren field
Frozen with snow.

Langston Hughes

16 Tons

Some people say a man is made outta mud
A poor man's made outta muscle and blood
Muscle and blood and skin and bones
A mind that's a-weak and a back that's strong

You load 16 tons, what you get?
Another day older and deeper in debt
St. Peter, don't you call me 'cause I can't go
I owe my soul to the company store

I was born one mornin' when the sun didn't shine
I picked up my shovel and I walked to the mine
I loaded 16 tons of number nine coal
And the straw boss said, "well a-bless my soul"

You Load 16 tons. Etc.

I was born one mornin', it was drizzling rain
Fighting and trouble are my middle name
I was raised in the canebreak by an ol' mama lion
Can't no high toned woman make me walk the line

You Load 16 tons. Etc.

If you see me comin', better step aside
A lotta men didn't, a lot of men died
One fist of iron, the other of steel
If the right one don't get you
Then the left one will

You Load 16 tons. Etc.

Merle Travis & Tennessee Ernie Ford

Sonnet 18: Shall I compare thee to a summer's day?

Shall I compare the to a summer's day?
Thou art more lovely and more temperate:
Rough winds do shake the darling buds of May,
And Summer's lease hath all too short a date;
Sometime too hot the eye of heaven shines,
And often in his gold complexion dimm'd;
And every fair from fair sometime declines,
By chance or nature's changing course untrimm'd;
But thy eternal summer shall not fade,
Nor lose possession of that fair thou ow'st;
Nor shall death brag thou wander'st in his shade,
When in eternal lines to time thou grow'st;
So long as men can breathe or eyes can see,
So long lives this, and this gives life to thee.

William Shakespeare

Sonnet 19: When I consider how my light is spent

When I consider how my light is spent,
Ere half my days, in this dark world and wide,
And that one Talent which is death to hide
Lodged with me useless, though my Soul more bent
To serve therewith my Maker, and present
My true account, lest he returning chide;
"Doth God exact day-labor, light denied?"
I fondly ask. But patience, to prevent
That murmur, soon replies, "God does not need
Either man's work or his own gifts; who best
Bear his mild yoke, they serve him best. His state
Is kingly. Thousands at his bidding speed
And post o'er Land and Ocean without rest:
they also serve who only stand and wait."

John Milton

Daffodils

I wandered lonely as a cloud
That floats on high o're vales and hills,
When all at once I saw a crowd,
A host, of golden daffodils;
Beside the lake, beneath the trees,
fluttering and dancing in the breeze.

Continuous as the stars that shine
And twinkle on the Milky Way,
They stretched in never-ending line
Along the margin of a bay:
Ten thousand saw I at a glance,
Tossing their heads in sprightly dance.

The waves beside them danced; but they
Out-did the sparkling waves in glee:
A poet could not but be gay,
In such a jocund company:
I gazed—and gazed—but little thought
What wealth the show to me had brought:

For oft, when my couch I lie
In vacant or in pensive mood,
They flash upon that inward eye
Which is the bliss of solitude;
And then my heart with pleasure fills,
And dances with the daffodils.

William Wordsworth

Fog

The fog comes
on little cat feet.

It sits looking
over harbor and city
on silent haunches
and then moves on.

Carl Sandberg

O Danny Boy

O Danny Boy, the pipes, the pipes are calling
From Glenn to Glen, and down the mountainside.
The summer's gone, and all the roses falling.
'Tis you, 'tis you must go and I must bide.
But come ye back when summer's in the meadow,
Or all the valley's hushed and white with snow.
'Tis I'll be here in sunshine or in shadow.
O, Danny Boy, O Danny Boy I love you so.

When winter's come, and all the flow'rs are dying,
If I am dead, as dead I well may be ,
You'll come and find the place where I am lying
And kneel and say an "Ave" there for me.

But I shall hear, though soft you tread above me,
And all my grave will warmer, sweeter be.
And you will bend and tell me that you love me;
And I shall sleep in peace until you come to me

Oh Danny Boy, the stream flows cool and slowly;
And pipes still call and echo 'cross the glen.
Your broken mother sighs and feels so lowly,
For you have not returned to smile again.

So if you've died and crossed the stream before us,
We pray that angels met you on the shore
And you'll look down, and gently you'll implore us
To live so we may see your smiling face once more,
Once more.

McKay Crockett & Evans Keith McKay

To Thine Own Self Be True

"This above all: to thine own self be true,
And it must follow, as the night the day,
Thou canst not then be false to any man.
Farewell, my blessing season this in thee!"

William Shakespeare, "Hamlet"

How Sharper

"How sharper than a serpent's tooth it is
To have a thankless child!"

William Shakespeare, "King Lear"

Cowards

"Cowards die many times before their deaths;
The valiant never taste of death but once.
Of all the wonders that I yet have heard,
It seems to me most strange that men should fear;
Seeing that death, a necessary end,
Will come when it will come."

William Shakespeare, "Julius Caesar"

Barbara Frietchie

Up from the Meadows rich with corn,
Clear in the cool September morn,

The clustered spires of Frederick stand
Green-walled by the hills of Maryland.

Round about them larger sweep,
Apple- and peach-tree fruited deep,

Fair as a garden of the Lord
To the eyes of the famished rebel horde,

On that pleasant morn of the early fall
When Lee marched over the mountain wall,—

Over the mountains winding down,
Horse and foot, into Frederick town,

Forty flags with their silver stars,
Forty flags with their crimson bars,

Flapped in the morning wind: the sun
Of noon looked down, and saw not one.

Up rose old Barbara Frietchie then,
Bowed with her fourscore years and ten;

Bravest of all in Frederick town,
She took up the flag and the men hauled down;

In her attic window the staff she set,
To show that one heart was loyal yet.

Up the street came to rebel tread,
Stonewall Jackson riding ahead.

Under his slouched hat left and right
He glanced: the old flag met his sight.

"Halt!" — the dust-brown ranks stood fast.

" Fire!" — out blazed the rifle-blast.

It shivered the window, the pane and sash;
It rent the banner with seam and gash.

Quick, as it fell, from the broken staff
Dame Barbara snatched the silken scarf;

She leaned far out on the window-sill,
And shook it forth with royal will.

"Shoot, if you must, this old gray head,
But spare your country's flag," she said.

A shade of sadness, a blush of shame,
Over the face of the leader came;

The nobler nature within him stirred
To life at that woman's deed and word:

"Who touches a hair of yon gray head
Dies like a dog! March on!" he said.

All day long through Frederick street
Sounded the tread of marching feet:

Ever its torn folds rose and fell
On the loyal winds that loved it well;

And through the light hill-gaps sunset light
Shown over it with a warm good-night.

Barbara Frietchie's work is o'er,
And the Rebel rides on his raids no more.

Honor to her! and let a tear
Fall, for her sake, on Stonewall's bier.

Over Barbara Frietchie's grave
Flag of Freedom and Union, wave!

Peace and order and beauty draw
Round thy symbol of light and law;

And ever the stars above look down
On thy stars below in Frederick town!

John Greenleaf Whittier

My Feet Are Wearied

"My feet are wearied, and my hands are tired,
My soul oppressed —

And I desire, what I have long desired —
Rest — only rest....

And so I cry, a weak and human cry,
For rest — for rest.

And so I sigh, a weak and human sigh,
For rest — for rest."

Father Abram J Ryan

Juliet's Speech

O Romeo, Romeo! Wherefore art thou Romeo?
Deny thy father and refuse thy name;
Or, if thou wilt not, be but sworn my love,
And I'll no longer be a Capulet....

'Tis but thy name that is my enemy;
Thou art thyself, though not a Montague.
What's Montague? it is nor hand, nor foot,
Nor arm, nor face, nor any other part
Belonging to a man. O, be some other name!
What's in a name? that which we call a rose
By any other name would smell as sweet;
So Romeo would, were he not Romeo call'd...

William Shakespeare, "Romeo and Juliet"

My kingdom for a horse!

King Richard III: "A horse! a horse! my kingdom for a horse!"

Catesby: "Withdraw, my lord; I'll help you to a horse."

King Richard III: "Slave, I have set my life upon a cast,
And I will stand the hazard of the die:
I think there be six Richmonds in the field;
Five have I slain to-day instead of him.
A horse! a horse! my kingdom for a horse!"

William Shakespeare, "Richard III"

Teddy Roosevelt One-liners #1

"Far and away the best prize that life has to offer is the chance to work hard at work worth doing."

"The only man who never makes a mistake is the man who never does anything."

"To educate a man in mind and not in morals is to educate a menace to society."

Teddy Roosevelt

Death, Be Not Proud

Death, be not proud, though some have called thee
Mighty and dreadful, for thou are not so;
For those whom thou think'st thou dost overthrow
Die not, poor Death, nor yet canst thou kill me.
From rest and sleep, which but thy pictures be,
Much pleasure; then from thee much more must flow,
And soonest our best men with thee do go,
Rest of their bones, and soul's delivery.
Thou art slave to fate, chance, kings, and desperate men,
And dost with poison, war, and sickness dwell,
And poppy or charms can make us sleep as well
And better than thy stroke; why swell'st thou then?
One short sleep past, we wake eternally
And death shall be no more; Death, thou shalt die.

John Donne

To Sleep

O soft embalmer of the still midnight,
 Shutting, with careful fingers and benign,
Our gloom-pleas'd eyes, empower'd from the light,
 Enshaded in forgetfulness divine:
  O soothest Sleep! if so it please thee, close
   In midst of this thine hymn my willing eyes,
   Or wait the "Amen," ere thy poppy throws
    Around my bed its lulling charities.
   Then save me, or the past day will shine
    Upon my pillow, breeding many woes —
Save me from curious Conscience, that still lords
 Its strength for darkness, burrowing like a mole;
  Turn the key deftly in the oiled wards,
  And seal the hushed Casket of my Soul.

John Keats

Mark Antony's Speech

Friends, Romans, countrymen, lend me your ears;
I come to bury Caesar, not to praise him.
The evil that men do lives after them;
The good is oft interred with their bones;
So let it be with Caesar. The noble Brutus
Hath told you Caesar was ambitious:
If it were so, it was a grievous fault,
And grievously had Caesar answer'd it.
Here, under leave of Brutus and the rest—
For Brutus is an honorable man;
So are they all, all honorable men—

Come I to speak in Caesar's funeral.
He was my friend, faithful and just to me:
But Brutus says he was ambitious;
And Brutus is an honorable man.
He hath brought many captives home to Rome
Whose ransoms and did the general coffers fill;
Did this in Caesar seem ambitious?
When that the poor have cried, Caesar hath wept;
Ambition should be made of sterner stuff:
Yet Brutus says he was ambitious;
And Brutus is an honorable man.
You all did see that on the Lupercal
I thrice presented him a kingly crown,
Which he did thrice refuse: was this ambition?
Yet Brutus says he was ambitious;
And, sure, he is an honorable man.
I speak not to disprove what Brutus spoke,
But here I am to speak what I do know.
You all did love him once, not without cause:
What cause withholds you then, to mourn for him?

O judgment! thou art fled to brutish beasts,
And men have lost their reason! —Bear with me;
My heart is in the coffin there with Caesar,
And I must pause till it come back to me.

William Shakespeare, "Julius Caesar"

To a Mouse on Turning Her Up in Her Nest with the Plough

November, 1785

Sleek, tiny, timorous, cowering beast,
Why's such panic in your breast?
Why dash away, so quick, so rash,
In a frenzied flash
When I would be loath to run after you
With a murderous plowstaff!

I'm truly sorry man's dominion
Has broken Nature's social union,
And justifies that bad opinion
Which makes you startle,
When I'm your poor, earth-bound companion
And fellow mortal!

I have no doubt you sometimes thieve;
What of it, friend? You too must live!
A random corn-ear in a shock's
A small behest; it'll give me a blessing to know such a loss;
I'll never miss it!

Your tiny house lies in a ruin,
Its fragile walls wind-rent and strewn!
Now nothing's left to construct you a new one
Of mosses green
Since bleak December's winds, ensuing,
Blow fast and keen!

You saw your fields laid bare and waste
With weary winter closing fast,
And cozy here, beneath the blast,

You thought to dwell,
Till crash! The cruel iron ploughshare passed
Straight through your cell!

That flimsy heap of leaves and stubble
Had cost you many a weary nibble!
Now you're turned out, for all your trouble,
Less house and hold,
To endure the winter's icy dribble
And hoarfrosts cold!

But mouse-friend, you are not alone
In proving foresight may be vain:
The best-laid schemes of Mice and Men
Go oft awry,
And leave us only grief and pain,
For promised joy!

Still, friend, you're blessed compared with me!
Only present dangers make you flee:
But, ouch!, behind me I can see
Grim prospects drear!
While forward-looking seers, we
Humans guess and fear!

Robert Burns

Teddy Roosevelt One-liners #2

"In any moment of decision, the best thing you can do is the right thing, the next best thing is the wrong thing, and the worst thing you can do is nothing."

"Speak softly and carry a big stick; you will go far."

"With self-discipline most anything is possible."

"It is hard to fail, but it is worse never to have tried to succeed."

"A vote is like a rifle; its usefulness depends upon the character of the user."

Teddy Roosevelt

The Lamb

Little lamb, who made thee?
Dost thou know who may thee,
Gave thee life, and bid thee feed
By the stream and o're the mead;

Gave thee clothing of the delight,
Softest clothing, woolly bright;
Gave thee such a tender voice,
Making all the vales rejoice?

Little lamb who made thee?
Dost thou know who made thee?

Little lamb, I'll tell thee;
Little lamb, I'll tell thee:
He is called by thy name,

For He calls himself a lamb.
He is meek, and He is mild,
He became a little child.

I a child, and thou a lamb,
We are called by His name.
Little lamb, God bless thee!
Little lamb, God bless thee!

William Blake, "The Lamb"

Man in The Arena

"It is not the critic who counts; not the man who points out how the strong man stumbles, or where the doer of deeds could have done them better. The credit belongs to the man who is actually in the arena, whose face is marred by dust and sweat and blood; who strives valiantly; who errs, who comes short again and again, because there is no effort without error and shortcoming; but who does actually strive to do the deeds; who knows great enthusiasms, the great devotions; who spends himself in a worthy cause; who at the best knows in the end the triumph of high achievement, and who at the worst, if he fails, at least fails while daring greatly, so that his place shall never be with those cold and timid souls who neither know victory nor defeat."

Teddy Roosevelt

Shakespeare One-liners #1

"The lady doth protest too much, methinks."

"Now is the winter of our discontent."

"Beware the ides of March."

"All that glitters is not gold."

"The better part of valor is discretion."

"Brevity is the soul of wit."

"Out, damn spot! out I say!"

"Lord, we know what we are, but know not what we may be."

Shakespeare

Father Malloy

You are over there, Father Malloy,
Where holy ground is, and the cross marks every grave,
Not here with us on the hill —
Us of wavering faith, and clouded vision
And drifting hope, and unforgiven sins.
You are so human, Father Malloy,
Taking a friendly glass sometimes with us,
Siding with us who would rescue Spoon River
From the coldness and the dreariness of village morality.
You were like a traveler who brings a little box of sand
From the wastes about the pyramids
And makes them real and Egypt real.
You were a part of and related to a great past,
And yet you were so close to many of us.
You believed in the joy of life.
You did not seem to be ashamed of the flesh.
You faced life as it is, and as it changes.

Some of us almost came to you, Father Malloy,
Seeing how your church had divined the heart,
And provided for it,
Through Peter the Flame,
Peter the rock

Edgar Lee Masters

God Bless America

God bless America, land that I love
Stand beside her and guide her
Through the night with the light from above

From the mountains to the prairies
To the oceans white with foam
God bless America, my home sweet home

God bless America, my home sweet home

Irving Berlin

Meditation 17

(This bell tolling softly for another, says to me,
Thou must die.)

Perchance he for whom this bell tolls may be so ill as that he knows not it tolls for him. And perchance I may think myself so much better than I am, as that they who are about me, and see my state, may have caused it to toll for me, and I know not that. The church is catholic, universal, so are all her actions; all that she does, belongs to all. When she baptizes a child, that action concerns me; for that child is thereby connected to that head which is my head too, and ingraffed into that body, whereof I am a member. And when she buries a man, that action concerns me; all mankind is of one author, and is one volume; when one man dies, one chapter is not torn out of the book, but translated into a better language; and every chapter must be so translated; God employs several translators; some pieces are translated by age, some by sickness, some by war, some by justice; but God's hand is in every translation, and his hand shall bind up all our scattered leaves again, for that library where every book shall lie open to one another; as therefore the bell that rings to a sermon, calls not upon the preacher only, but upon the congregation to come; so this bell calls us all: but how much more me, who am brought so near the door by this sickness.

There was a contention as far as a suit (in which, piety and dignity, religion and estimation, were mingled) which of the religious orders should ring to prayers first in the morning; and it was determined, that they should ring first that rose earliest. If we understand aright the dignity of this bell, that tolls for our evening prayer, we would be glad to make it ours, by rising early, in that application, that it might be ours as well as his, whose indeed it is. The bell doth toll for him, that thinks it doth; and though it intermit again, yet from that minute, that that occasion wrought upon him, he is united to God. Who casts not up his eye to the sun when it rises? But who takes off his eye from a comet, when that breaks out? who bends not his ear to any bell, which upon any occasion rings? But who can remove it from that bell, which is passing a piece of himself out of this world?

No man is an island, entire of itself; every man is a piece of the continent, a part of the main; if a clod be washed away by the sea, Europe is the less, as well as if a promontory were, as well as if a manor of thy friend's or of thine own were; any man's death diminishes me, because I am involved in mankind, and therefore never send to know for whom the bell tolls; it tolls for thee.

Neither can we call this a begging of misery, or a borrowing of misery, as though we were not miserable enough of ourselves, but must fetch in more from the next house, in taking upon us the misery of our neighbors. Truly it were an excusable covetousness if we did; for affliction is a treasure, and scarce any man hath enough of it. No man hath afflicion enough, that is not matured and ripened by it, and made fit for God by that affliction. If a man carry treasure in bullion or in a wedge of gold, and have none coined into current moneys, his treasure will not defray him as he travels. Tribulation is treasure in the nature of it, but it is not current money in the use of it, except we get nearer and nearer our home, heaven, by it. Another may be sick too, and sick to death, and this affliction may lie in his bowels, as gold in a mine, and be of no use to him; but this bell that tells me of his affliction, digs out, and applies that gold to me: if by this consideration of another's danger, I take mine own into contemplation, and so secure myself, by making my recourse to my God, who is our only security.

John Donne

The Hill

Where are Elmer, Herman, Bert, Tom and Charley,
The weak of will, the strong of arm, the clown, the boozer, the fighter?
All, all are sleeping on the hill.

One passed in a fever,
One was burned in a mine,
One was killed in a brawl,
One died in a jail,
One fell from a bridge toiling for children and wife —
All, all are sleeping, sleeping, sleeping on the hill.

Where are Ella, Kate, Mag, Lizzie and Edith,
The tender heart, the simple soul, the loud, the proud, the happy one? —
All, all are sleeping on the hill.

One died in shameful child-birth,
One of a thwarted love,
One at the hands of a brute in a brothel,
One of a broken pride, in the search for heart's desire,
One after life in far-away London and Paris
Was brought to her little space by Ella and Kate and Mag —
All, all are sleeping, sleeping, sleeping on the hill.

Where are Uncle Isaac and Aunt Emily,
And old Towny Kincaid and Sevigne Houghton,
And Major Walker who had talked
With venerable men of the revolution? —
All, all are sleeping on the hill.

They brought them dead sons from the war,
And daughters whom life had crushed,

And their children fatherless, crying —
All, all are sleeping, sleeping, sleeping on the hill.

Where is Old Fiddler Jones
Who played with life all his ninety years,
Braving the sleet with bared breast,
Drinking, rioting, thinking neither of wife nor kin,
Nor gold, nor love, nor heaven?
Lo! he babbles of the fish-frys of long ago,
Of the horse-races of long ago at Clary's Grove,
Of what Abe Lincoln said
One time at Springfield.

Edgar Lee Masters

Teddy Roosevelt One-liners #3

"A thorough knowledge of the Bible is worth more than a college education."

"The most important single ingredient in the formula of success is knowing how to get along with people."

Teddy Roosevelt

Charge of the Light Brigade

I

Half a league, half a league,
Half a league onward,
All in the valley of Death
Rode the six hundred.
"Forward, the Light Brigade!
Charge for the guns!" he said.
Into the valley of Death
Rode the six hundred.

II

"Forward, the Light Brigade!"
Was there a man dismayed?
Not though the soldier knew
Someone had blundered.
Theirs not to make reply,
Theirs not to reason why,
Theirs but to do and die.
Into the valley of Death
Rode the six hundred.

III

Cannon to right of them,
Cannon to left of them,
Cannon in front of them
Volleyed and thundered;
Stormed at with shot and shell,
Boldly they rode and well,
Into the jaws of Death,
Into the mouth of hell
Rode the six hundred.

IV

Flashed all their sabres bare,
Flashed as they turned in air
Sabring the gunners there,
Charging an army, while
All the world wondered.
Plunged in the battery-smoke
Right through the line they broke;
Cossack and Russian
Reeled from the sabre stroke
Shattered and sundered.
Then they rode back, but not
Not the six hundred.

V

Cannon to right of them,
Cannon to left of them,
Cannon behind them
Volleyed and thundered;
Stormed at with shot and shell,
While horse and hero fell.
They that had fought so well
Came through the jaws of Death,
Back from the mouth of hell,
All that was left of them,
Left of six hundred.

VI

When can their glory fade?
O the wild charge they made!
All the world wondered.
Honour the charge they made!
Honour the Light Brigade,
Noble six hundred!

Alfred, Lord Tennyson

Lucinda Matlock

I went to the dances at Chandlerville,
And played snap-out at Winchester.
One time we changed partners,
Driving home in the moonlight of middle June,
And then I found Davis.
We were married and lived together for seventy years,
Enjoying, working, raising the twelve children,
Eight of whom we lost
Ere I had reached the age of sixty.
I spun, I wove, I kept the house, I nursed the sick,
I made the garden, and for holiday
Rambled over the fields where sang the larks,
And by Spoon River gathering many a shell,
And many a flower and medicinal weed —
Shouting to the wooded hills, singing to the green valleys.
At ninety-six I had lived enough, that is all,
And passed to a sweet repose.
What is this I hear of sorrow and weariness,
Anger, discontent, and drooping hopes?
Degenerate sons and daughters,
Life is too strong for you —
It takes life to love Life.

Edgar Lee Masters

Pledge of Allegiance

"I pledge allegiance to the flag of the United
States of America, and to the Republic for which it
stands, one Nation under God, indivisible,
with liberty and justice for all
with liberty justice for all."

Francis Bellamy

Teddy Roosevelt One-liners #4

"We can have no '50-50' allegiance in this country. Either a man is an American and nothing else, or he is not an American at all."

"Order without liberty and liberty without order are equally destructive."

"Great thoughts speak only to the thoughtful mind, but great actions speak to all mankind."

Teddy Roosevelt

Trees

I think that I shall never see
A poem lovely as a tree.

A tree whose hungry mouth is prest
Against the earth's sweet flowing breast;

A tree that looks at God all day,
And lifts her leafy arms to pray;

A tree that may in Summer wear
A nest of robins in her hair;

Upon whose bosom snow has lain;
Who intimately lives with rain.

Poems are made by fools like me,
But only God can make a tree.

Joyce Kilmer

O Captain! My Captain

O Captain! my Captain! our fearful trip is done,
The ship has weather'd every rack, the prize we sought is won,
The port is near, the bells I hear, the people all exulting,
While follow eyes the steady keel, the vessel grim and daring;
But O heart! heart! heart!
O the bleeding drops of red,
Where on the deck my Captain lies,
Fallen cold and dead.

O Captain! my Captain! rise up and hear the bells;
Rise up—for you the flag is flung—for you the bugle trills,
For you bouquets and ribbon'd wreaths—for you the shores a-crowding,
For you they call, the swaying mass, their eager faces turning;
Here Captain! dear father!
This arm beneath your head!
It is some dream that on the deck,
You've fallen cold and dead.

My Captain does not answer, his lips are pale and still,
My father does not feel my arm, he has no pulse nor will,
The ship is anchor'd safe and sound, its voyage closed and done,
From fearful trip the victor ship comes in with object won;
Exult O shores, and ring O bells!
But I with mournful tread,
Walk the deck my Captain lies,
Fallen cold and dead.

Walt Whitman

To a Louse, On Seeing One on a Lady's Bonnet at Church

(Standard English Translation)

Ha! Where are you going, you crawling wonder?
Your impudence protects you sorely,
I cannot say but you swagger rarely
Over gauze and lace,
Though faith! I fear you dine but sparingly
On such a place.

You ugly, creeping, blasted wonder,
Detested, shunned by saint and sinner,
How dare you set your foot upon her –
Such fine a lady!
Go somewhere else and seek your dinner
On some poor body

Off! in some beggar's temples squat:
There you may creep, and sprawl, and scramble,
With other kindred, jumping cattle,
In shoals and nations;
Where horn nor bone never dare unsettle
Your thick plantations

Now hold you there! you are out of sight,
Below the falderals, snug and tight;
No, faith you yet! you will not be right,
Until you have got on it ---
The very topmost, towering height
Of misses bonnet.

My sooth! right bold you set your nose out,
As plump and gray as any gooseberry:

O for some rank, mercurial resin,
Or deadly, red powder,
I would give you such a hearty dose of it,
Would dress your breech!

I would not have been surprised to spy
You on an old wife's flannel cap:
Or maybe some small ragged boy,
On his undervest;
But Miss's fine balloon bonnet! fye!
How dare you do it.

O Jenny do not toss your head,
And set your beauties all abroad!
You little know what cursed speed
The blastie's making!
Those winks and finger-ends, I dread,
Are notice taking!

O would some Power the gift to give us
To see ourselves as others see us!
It would from many a blunder free us,
And foolish notion:
What airs in dress and gait would leave us,
And even devotion!

Robert Burns

St. Crispian's Day Speech

WESTMORELAND
O that we now had here
But one ten thousand of those men in England
That do no work to-day!

KING HENRY V
What's he that wishes so?
My cousin Westmoreland? No, my fair cousin:
If we are mark'd to die, we are enow
To do our country loss; and if to live,
The fewer men, the greater share of honour.
God's will! I pray thee, wish not one man more.
By Jove, I am not covetous for gold,
Nor care I who doth feed upon my cost;
It yearns me not if men my garments wear;
Such outward things dwell not in my desires:
But if it be a sin to covet honour,
I am the most offending soul alive.
No, faith, my coz, wish not a man from England:
God's peace! I would not lose so great an honour
As one man more, methinks, would share from me
For the best hope I have. O, do not wish one more!
Rather proclaim it, Westmoreland, through my host,
That he which hath no stomach to this fight,
Let him depart; his passport shall be made
And crowns for convoy put into his purse:
We would not die in that man's company
That fears his fellowship to die with us.
This day is called the feast of Crispian:
He that outlives this day, and comes safe home,
Will stand a tip-toe when this day is named,
And rouse him at the name of Crispian.

He that shall live this day, and see old age,
Will yearly on the vigil feast his neighbours,
And say 'To-morrow is Saint Crispian:'
Then will he strip his sleeve and show his scars.
And say 'These wounds I had on Crispin's day.'
Old men forget: yet all shall be forgot,
But he'll remember with advantages
What feats he did that day: then shall our names.
Familiar in his mouth as household words
Harry the king, Bedford and Exeter,
Warwick and Talbot, Salisbury and Gloucester,
Be in their flowing cups freshly remember'd.
This story shall the good man teach his son;
And Crispin Crispian shall ne'er go by,
From this day to the ending of the world,
But we in it shall be remember'd;
We few, we happy few, we band of brothers;
For he to-day that sheds his blood with me
Shall be my brother; be he ne'er so vile,
This day shall gentle his condition:
And gentlemen in England now a-bed
Shall think themselves accursed they were not here,
And hold their manhoods cheap whiles any speaks
That fought with us upon Saint Crispin's day.

William Shakespeare

Casey at the Bat

(A Ballad of the Republic, Sung in the Year 1888)

The outlook wasn't brilliant for the Mudville nine that day;
The score stood four to two with but one inning more to play.
And then when Cooney died at first, and Barrows did the same,
A sickly silence fell upon the patrons of the game.

A straggling few got up to go in deep despair. The rest
Clung to that hope which springs eternal in the human breast;
They thought if only Casey could but get a whack at that—
We'd put up even money now with Casey at the bat.

But Flynn preceded Casey, as did also Jimmy Blake,
And the former was a lulu and the latter was a cake;
So upon that stricken multitude grim melancholy sat,
For there seemed but little chance of Casey's getting to the bat.

But Flynn let drive a single, to the wonderment of all,
And Blake, the much despised, tore the cover off the ball;
And when the dust had lifted, and men saw what had occurred,
There was Jimmy safe at second and Flynn a-hugging third.

Then from 5,000 throats and more there rose a lusty yell;
It rumbled through the valley, it rattled in the dell;
It knocked upon the mountain and recoiled upon the flat,
For Casey, mighty Casey, was advancing to the bat.

There was ease in Casey's manner as he stepped into his place;
There was pride in Casey's bearing and a smile on Casey's face.
And when, responding to the cheers, he lightly doffed his hat,
No stranger in the crowd could doubt 'twas Casey at the bat.

Ten thousand eyes were on him as he rubbed his hands with dirt;

Five thousand tongues applauded when he wiped them on his shirt.
Then while the writhing pitcher ground the ball into his hip,
Defiance gleamed in Casey's eye, a sneer curled Casey's lip.

And now the leather-covered sphere came hurtling through the air,
And Casey stood a-watching it in haughty grandeur there.
Close by the sturdy batsman the ball unheeded sped—
"That ain't my style," said Casey. "Strike one," the umpire said.

From the benches, black with people, there went up a muffled roar,
Like the beating of the storm-waves on a stern and distant shore.
"Kill him! Kill the umpire!" shouted some one on the stand;
And it's likely they'd have killed him had not Casey raised his hand.

With a smile of Christian charity great Casey's visage shone;
He stilled the rising tumult; he bade the game go on;
He signaled to the pitcher, and once more the spheroid flew;
But Casey still ignored it, and the umpire said, "Strike two."

"Fraud!" cried the maddened thousands, and echo answered fraud;
But one scornful look from Casey and the audience was awed.
They saw his face grow stern and cold, they saw his muscles strain,
And they knew that Casey wouldn't let that ball go by again.

The sneer is gone from Casey's lip, his teeth are clinched in hate;
He pounds with cruel violence his bat upon the plate.
And now the pitcher holds the ball, and now he lets it go,
And now the air is shattered by the force of Casey's blow.

Oh, somewhere in this favored land the sun is shining bright;
The band is playing somewhere, and somewhere hearts are light,
And somewhere men are laughing, and somewhere children shout;
But there is no joy in Mudville—mighty Casey has struck out.

Ernest Lawrence Thayer

In The Land Where We Were Dreaming

    FAIR were our visions! Oh, they were as grand
        As ever floated out of faerie land;
        Children were we in single faith,
        But God-like children, whom nor death
Nor threat nor danger drove from honor's path,   5
        In the land where we were dreaming.

    Proud were our men, as pride of birth could render;
        As violets, our women pure and tender;
        And when they spoke, their voices did thrill
        Until at eve the whip-poor-will,   10
At morn the mocking-bird, were mute and still,
        In the land where we were dreaming.

And we had graves that covered more of glory
        Than ever tracked tradition's ancient story;
        And in our dream we wove the thread   15
        Of principles for which had bled
    And suffered long our own immortal dead,
        In the land where we were dreaming.

    Though in our land we had both bond and free,
Both were content; and so God let them be;—   20
        'Till envy coveted our land,
        And those fair fields our valor won;
    But little recked we, for we still slept on,
        In the land where we were dreaming.

Our sleep grew troubled and our dreams grew wild—   25
    Red meteors flashed across our heaven's field;
        Crimson the moon; between the Twins
        Barbed arrows fly, and then begins

Such strife as when disorder's Chaos reigns,
    In the land where we were dreaming.

Down from her sun-lit heights smiled Liberty
    And waved her cap in sign of Victory—
    The world approved, and everywhere,
    Except where growled the Russian bear,
The good, the brave, the just gave us their prayer   35
    In the land where we were dreaming.

We fancied that a Government was ours—
We challenged place among the world's great powers;
    We talked in sleep of Rank, Commission,
    Until so life-like grew our vision   40
That he who dared to doubt but met derision,
    In the land where we were dreaming.

We looked on high: a banner there was seen,
Whose field was blanched and spotless in its sheen—
    Chivalry's cross its Union bears,   45
    And veterans swearing by their scars
Vowed they would bear it through a hundred wars,
    In the land where we were dreaming.

A hero came amongst us as we slept;
At first he lowly knelt—then rose and wept;   50
    Then gathering up a thousand spears
    He swept across the field of Mars;
Then bowed farewell and walked beyond the stars,
    In the land where we were dreaming.

We looked again: another figure still   55
Gave hope, and nerved each individual will—
    Full of grandeur, clothed with power,
    Self-poised, erect, he ruled the hour

With stern, majestic sway—of strength a tower,
    In the land where we were dreaming. 60

As, while great Jove, in bronze, a warder God,
Gazed eastward from the Forum where he stood,
    Rome felt herself secure and free,
   So, "Richmond's safe," we said, while we
  Beheld a bronzéd hero—God-like Lee,   65
    In the land where we were dreaming.

As wakes the soldier when the alarum calls—
  As wakes the mother when the infant falls—
    As starts the traveler when around
  His sleeping couch the fire-bells sound—   70
   So woke our nation with a single bound,
    In the land where we were dreaming.

Woe! woe is me! the startled mother cried—
While we have slept our noble sons have died!
  Woe! woe is me! how strange and sad   75
    That all our glorious vision's fled,
  And left us nothing real but the dead,
    In the land where we were dreaming.

And are they really dead, our martyred slain?
No, Dreamers! Morn shall bid them rise again,
    From every plain, -- from every height, --
    On which they seemed to die for right,
  Their gallant spirits shall renew the fight,
    In the land where we were dreaming!

Unconquered still in soul, tho' now o'er-run,
  In peace, in war, the battle's just begun!
    Once this Thyestean banquet o'er,
  Grown strong the few who bide their hour,

Shall rise and hurl its drunken guests from power,
In the land where we were dreaming!

Daniel Lucas

Prayer, and Hope of Victory

Now may the God of grace and power
Attend his people's humble cry;
Defend them in the needful hour,
And send deliverance from on high.

In His salvation is our hope;
And in the name of Israel's God
Our troops shall lift their banners up,
Our navies spread their flags abroad.

Some trust in horses trained for war,
And some of chariots make their boast;
Our surest expectations are
From Thee, the Lord of heavenly hosts.

Then save us, Lord, from slavish fear,
And let our trust be firm and strong,
Till Thy salvation shall appear,
And hymns of peace conclude our song.

Charles Quintard

A Land Without Ruins

"A land without ruins is a land without memories —
a land without memories is a land without history.
A land that wears a laurel crown may be fair to see;
but twine a few sad cypress leaves around the brow of any land,
and be that land barren, beautiless and bleak, it becomes lovely
in its consecrated coronet of sorrow, and it wins the sympathy of the heart
and of history. Crowns of roses fade — crowns of thorns endure.
Calvaries and crucifixions take deepest hold of humanity —
the triumphs of might are transient — they pass and are forgotten —
the sufferings of right are graven deepest on the chronicle of nations."

Yes give me the land where the ruins are spread,
And the living tread light on the hearts of the dead;
Yes, give me a land that is blest by the dust,
And bright with the deeds of the down-trodden just.
Yes, give me the land where the battle's red blast
Has flashed to the future the fame of the past;
Yes, give me the land that hath legends and lays
That tell of the memories of long vanished days;
Yes, give me a land that hath story and song!
Enshrine the strife of the right with the wrong!
Yes, give me a land with a grave in each spot,
And names in the graves that shall not be forgot;
Yes, give me the land of the wreck and the tomb;
There is grandeur in graves — there is glory in gloom;
For out of the gloom future brightness is born,
As after the night comes the sunrise of morn;
And the graves of the dead with the grass overgrown
May yet form the footstool of liberty's throne,
And each single wreck in the war path of might
Shall yet be a rock in the temple of right.

Abram Joseph Ryan

Hark to the Shouting Wind!

Hark to the shouting Wind!
Hark to the flying Rain!
And I care not though I never see
A bright blue sky again.

There are thoughts in my breast to-day
That are not for human speech;
But I hear them in the driving storm,
And the roar upon the beach.

And oh, to be with that ship
That I watch through the blinding brine!
O Wind! for thy sweep of land and sea!
O Sea! for a voice like thine!

Shout on, thou pitiless Wind,
To the frightened and flying Rain!
I care not though I never see
A calm blue sky again.

Henry Timrod

A Song of Eternity in Time

ONCE, at night, in the manor wood
My Love and I long silent stood,
Amazed that any heavens could
Decree to part us, bitterly repining.

My Love, in aimless love and grief,
Reached forth and drew aside a leaf
That just above us played the thief
And stole our starlight that for us was shining.
A star that had remarked her pain
Shone straightway down that leafy lane,
And wrought his image, mirror-plain,
Within a tear that on her lash hung gleaming.

"Thus Time," I cried, "is but a tear
Someone hath wept 'twixt hope and fear,
Yet in his little lucent sphere
Our star of stars, Eternity, is beaming."

Sidney Lanier

Fire and Ice

Some say the world will end in fire,
Some say in ice.
From what I've tasted of desire
I hold with those who favor fire.
But if it had to perish twice,
I think I know enough of hate
To say that for destruction ice
Is also great
And would suffice.

Robert Frost

Richard Cory

Whenever Richard Cory went down town,
We people on the pavement looked at him:
He was a gentleman from sole to crown,
Clean favored, and imperially slim.

And he was always quietly arrayed,
And he was always human when he talked;
But still he fluttered pulses when he said,
"Good-morning," and he glittered when he walked.

And he was rich — yes, richer than a king —
And admirably schooled in every grace:
In fine, we thought that he was everything
To make us wish that we were in his place.

So on we worked, and waited for the light,
And went without the meat, and cursed the bread;
And Richard Cory, one calm summer night,
Went home and put a bullet through his head.

Edwin Arlington Robinson

Tomorrow, and Tomorrow, and Tomorrow

Tomorrow, and tomorrow, and tomorrow,
Creeps in this petty pace from day to day,
To the last syllable of recorded time;
And all our yesterdays have lighted fools
The way to dusty death. Out, out, brief candle!
Life's but a walking shadow, a poor player,
That struts and frets his hour upon the stage,
And then is heard no more. It is a tale
Told by an idiot, full of sound and fury,
Signifying nothing.

William Shakespeare, "Macbeth"

Niccol Machiavelli One-liners

"Of mankind we may say in general they are fickle, hypocritical, and greedy of gain."

"One who deceives will always find those who allow themselves to be deceived."

"Everyone sees what you appear to be, few experience what you really are."

"The first method for estimating the intelligence Of a ruler is to look at the men he has around him."

"A government which does not trust its citizens to be armed is not itself to be trusted."

"It is better to act and repent than not to act and regret."

"Power is the pivot on which everything hinges. He who has the power is always right; the weaker is always wrong."

"A sign of intelligence is an awareness of one's own ignorance."

Niccol Machiavelli, "The Prince"

To the Virgins, to Make Much of Time

Gather ye rose-buds while ye may,
Old Time is still a-flying;
And this same flower that smiles today
Tomorrow will be dying.

The glorious lamp of heaven, the sun,
The higher he's a-getting,
The sooner will his race be run,
And nearer he's to setting.

That age is best which is the first,
When youth and blood are warmer;
But being spent, the worse, and worst
Times still succeed the former.

Then be not coy, but use your time,
And while ye may, go marry;
For having lost but once your prime,
You may forever tarry.

Robert Herrick

When You Are Old

When you are old and grey and full of sleep,
And nodding by the fire, take down this book,
And slowly read, and dream of the soft look
Your eyes had once, and of their shadows deep;

How many loved your moments of glad grace,
And loved your beauty with love false or true,
But one man loved the pilgrim soul in you,
And loved the sorrows of your changing face;

And bending down beside the glowing bars,
Murmur, a little sadly, how Love fled
And paced upon the mountains overhead
And hid his face amid a crowd of stars.

William Butler Yeats

Sonnet 116

Let me not to the marriage of true minds
Admit impediments. Love is not love
Which alters when it alteration finds,
Or bends with the remover to remove.
O no! it is an ever-fixed mark
That looks on tempests and is never shaken;
It is the star to every wand'ring bark,
Whose worth's unknown, although his height be taken.
Love's not Time's fool, though rosy lips and cheeks
Within his bending sickle's compass come;
Love alters not with his brief hours and weeks,
But bears it out even to the edge of doom.
If this be error and upon me prov'd,
I never writ, nor no man ever lov'd.

William Shakespeare

I carry your heart with me

I carry your heart with me (I carry it in
my heart) I am never without it (anywhere
I go you go, my dear; and whatever is done
by only me is your doing, my darling)

I fear no fate (for you are my fate, my sweet) I want
no world (for beautiful you are my world, my true)
and it's you are whatever a moon has always meant
and whatever a sun will always sing is you

Here is the deepest secret nobody knows
(here is the root of the root and the bud of the bud
and the sky of the sky of a tree called life; which grows
higher than soul can hope or mind can hide)
and this is the wonder that's keeping the stars apart

I carry your heart (I carry it in my heart)

E. E. Cummins

Judged By the Company One Keeps

One night in late October,
When I was far from sober,
Returning with my load With manly pride,
My feet began to stutter,
So I lay down in the gutter,
And a pig came near and lay down by my side;
A lady passing by was heard to say:
"You can tell a man who boozes,
By the company he chooses,"
And the pig got up and slowly walked away.

Anonymous

When I Too Long

When I too long have looked upon your face,
Wherein for me a brightness unobscured
Save by the mists of brightness has its place,
And terrible beauty not to be endured,
I turn away reluctant from your light,
And stand irresolute, a mind undone,
A silly, dazzled thing deprived of sight
From having looked too long upon the sun.
Then is my daily life a narrow room
In which a little while, uncertainly,
Surrounded by impenetrable gloom,
Among familiar things grown strange to me
Making my way, I pause, and feel, and hark,
Till I become accustomed to the dark.

Edna St. Vincent Millay

The Swing

How do you like to go up in a swing,
  Up in the air so blue?
Oh, I do think it the pleasantest thing
  Ever a child can do!

Up in the air and over the wall,
  Till I can see so wide,
Rivers and trees and cattle and all
  Over the countryside—

Till I look down on the garden green,
  Down on the roof so brown—
Up in the air I go flying again,
  Up in the air and down!

Robert Louis Stevenson

Who Has Seen the Wind?

Who has seen the wind?
Neither I nor you:
But when the leaves hang trembling,
The wind is passing through.

Who has seen the wind?
Neither you nor I:
But when the trees bow down their heads,
The wind is passing by.

Christina Rossetti

My Shadow

I have a little shadow that goes in and out with me,
And what can be the use of him is more than I can see.
He is very, very like me from the heels up to the head;
And I see him jump before me, when I jump into my bed.

The funniest thing about him is the way he likes to grow—
Not at all like proper children, which is always very slow;
For he sometimes shoots up taller like an india-rubber ball,
And he sometimes gets so little that there's none of him at all.

He hasn't got a notion of how children ought to play,
And can only make a fool of me in every sort of way.
He stays so close beside me, he's a coward you can see;
I'd think shame to stick to nursie as that shadow sticks to me!

One morning, very early, before the sun was up,
I rose and found the shining dew on every buttercup;
But my lazy little shadow, like an arrant sleepy-head,
Had stayed at home behind me and was fast asleep in bed.

Robert Louis Stevenson

The Owl and the Pussy-Cat

I

The Owl and the Pussy-cat went to sea
In a beautiful pea-green boat,
They took some honey, and plenty of money,
Wrapped up in a five-pound note.
The Owl looked up to the stars above,
And sang to a small guitar,
"O lovely Pussy! O Pussy, my love,
What a beautiful Pussy you are,
You are,
You are!
What a beautiful Pussy you are!"

II

Pussy said to the Owl, "You elegant fowl!
How charmingly sweet you sing!
O let us be married! too long we have tarried:
But what shall we do for a ring?"
They sailed away, for a year and a day,
To the land where the Bong-Tree grows
And there in a wood a Piggy-wig stood
With a ring at the end of his nose,
His nose,
His nose,
With a ring at the end of his nose.

III

"Dear Pig, are you willing to sell for one shilling
Your ring?" Said the Piggy, "I will."
So they took it away, and were married next day
By the Turkey who lives on the hill.
They dined on mince, and slices of quince,
Which they ate with a runcible spoon;
And hand in hand, on the edge of the sand,
They danced by the light of the moon,
The moon,
The moon,
They danced by the light of the moon.

Edward Lear

The Road Ahead

My Lord God,
I have no idea where I am going.
I do not see the road ahead of me.
I cannot know for certain where it will end.
nor do I really know myself,
and the fact that I think I am following your will
does not mean that I am actually doing so.
ButI believe that the desire to please you
does in fact please you.
And I hope I have that desire in all that I am doing.
I hope that I will never do anything apart from that desire.

And I know that if I do this you will lead me by the right road,

though I may know nothing about it.
Therefore will I trust you always though
I may seem to be lost and in the shadow of death.

I will not fear, for you are ever with me,
and you will never leave me to face my perils alone.

Thomas Merton, "Thoughts in Solitude"

Ronald Reagan One-liners #1

"Government exists to protect us from each other. Where government has gone beyond its limits is in Deciding to protect us from ourselves."

"I've noticed that everyone who is for abortion has already been born."

"The greatest leader is not necessarily the one who does the greatest things. He is the one that gets the people to do the greatest things."

"Freedom is never more than one generation away From extinction. We didn't pass it to our children in the bloodstream. It must be fought for, protected, and handed on for them to do the same, or one day we will spend our sunset years telling our children and our children's children what it was once like in the United States where men were free."

"If we ever forget that we're one nation under God, then we will be one nation gone under."

"Within the covers of the Bible are the answers for all the problems men face."

Ronald Reagan

Ronald Reagan One-liners #2

"There is no limit to the amount of good you can do if you don't care who gets the credit."

"As government expands, liberty contracts."

"The most terrifying words in the English language are: I'm from the government and I'm here to help."

"Christmas can be celebrated in the school room with Pine trees, tinsel and reindeers, but there must be no mention of the man whose birthday is being celebrated. One wonders how a teacher would answer if a student asked why it was called Christmas."

"Live simply, love generously, care deeply, speak kindly, leave the rest to God."

"Republicans believe every day is the Fourth of July, but the democrats believe every day is April 15."

"We must reject the idea that every time a law's broken, society is guilty rather than the lawbreaker. It is time to restore the American precept that each individual is accountable for his actions."

Ronald Reagan

The Windhover

To Christ our Lord

I caught this morning morning's minion, king-
dom of daylight's dauphin, dapple-dawn-drawn Falcon, in his riding
    Of the rolling level underneath him steady air, and striding
    High there, how he rung upon the rein of a wimpling wing
In his ecstasy! then off, off forth on swing,
As a skate's heel sweeps smooth on a bow-bend: the hurl and gliding
    Rebuffed the big wind. My heart in hiding
Stirred for a bird, – the achieve of, the mastery of the thing.

Brute beauty and valour and act, oh, air, pride, plume, here
    Buckle! AND the fire that breaks from thee then, a billion
Times told lovelier, more dangerous, O my chevalier!

No wonder of it: shéer plód makes plough down sillion
    Shine, and blue-bleak embers, ah my dear,
    Fall, gall themselves, and gash gold-vermilion.

Gerard Manley Hopkins

Ronald Reagan One-liners #3

"A nation that cannot control its borders is not a nation."

"I know in my heart that man is good, that what is right will always eventually triumph, and there is purpose and worth to each and every life."

"Government's view of the economy could be summed up in a few short phrases: If it moves, tax it. If it keeps moving, regulate it. And if it stops moving, subsidize it."

"I hope we once again have reminded people that man is not free unless government is limited.

There's a clear cause and effect here that is as neat and predictable as a law of physics: As government expands, liberty contracts."

"It isn't so much that liberals are ignorant. It's just that they know so many things that aren't so."

Ronald Reagan

Riddle of the World

Know then thyself, presume not God to scan;
The proper study of Mankind is Man.
Placed on this isthmus of a middle state,
A Being darkly wise, and rudely great:
With too much knowledge for the Sceptic side,
With too much weakness for the Stoic's pride,
He hangs between; in doubt to act, or rest;
In doubt to deem himself a God, or Beast;
In doubt his mind and body to prefer;
Born but to die, and reas'ning but to err;
Whether he thinks to little, or too much;
Chaos of Thought and Passion, all confus'd;
Still by himself, abus'd or disabus'd;
Created half to rise and half to fall;
Great Lord of all things, yet a prey to all,
Sole judge of truth, in endless error hurl'd;
The glory, jest and riddle of the world.

Alexander Pope

The Star-Spangled Banner

O say can you see, by the dawn's early light,
What so proudly we hail'd at the twilight's last gleaming,
Whose broad stripes and bright stars through the perilous fight
O'er the ramparts we watch'd were so gallantly streaming?
And the rocket's red glare, the bombs bursting in air,
Gave proof through the night that our flag was still there,
O say does that star-spangled banner yet wave
O'er the land of the free and the home of the brave?

Francis Scott Keys

Ronald Reagan One-liners #4

"Freedom prospers when religion is vibrant and the rule of law under God is acknowledged."

"Recession is when your neighbor loses his job. Depression is when you lose yours. And recovery is when Jimmy Carter loses his."

"Politics is not a bad profession. If you succeed there are many rewards, if you disgrace yourself you can always write a book."

Ronald Reagan

Weather

Ubiquitous weather you are changing all the time
To manifold seasons, you give your fealty as you please

Your sundry excesses cause calamity aplenty
While your habitual benevolence gives
Universal pleasure

Playing outside in the bright summertime sun
Then swirling air now quickly cooling – so fine
The dark cumulonimbus clouds are swiftly moving

The wind chills us before the drops are raining down
Barefoot we feel the grass between our toes
Prancing chaotically on our beautiful St Augustine
We spread our arms, looking skyward thirstily

We consume pure water, ambrosia from above
Huge ominous black clouds darken the sky
And alarming signs of lightning bolts so near
Their widespread tendrils we all did fear
So, we scurried inside to watch in safety dear

As much time passed, I learned new weather incites
Healing rain gives boost to my flowers bright
But pouring monsoons cause anxiety and fright
Floods and rising water threaten all we have

Winter, spring, summer, fall, we welcome all
The vagaries of weather make us smile or bawl
We suffer either favor, or unexpected turmoil
We must be vigilant, ready to adapt or fail

Family Reading Time

When we see the exquisite floating chevrons above
The elegant rhythmic geese are headed southward
Thus we ken, frigid winds will soon be here
I blanketed my plants to protect tender beauties

I hoped deep frost would surely stay afar
But it came with fury and too soon
My trust in garden covers was jejune
The frozen devastation was utterly pervasive

I found only crisp brown twigs, or soggy mush
Patiently I cut way back and waited still more
A few inhabitants revived, but most remained lifeless
Sadly, a coveted convivial result did not emerge

Weather let your expressions be extreme no more
Frost be light, and you are welcome here again
Abundant rain come down, but do not inundate us
Be clement summer climate, perpetuate no drought

Opportunities now arise to enliven and renew
New floral standouts I assiduously pursue
Unfamiliar forms and fresh colors did enchant
So, with these, efforts my oasis was restored

Climbing clematis, plumbago, multicolored irises
Butterfly bushes, liriope, splashing caladiums
Creeping thyme, wisteria, liatris, dusty miller
Honeysuckle, milkweed, and coneflower all entice

The tintinnabulation of windchimes all around
A wooden swing provides a perfect viewing forum
Mother Mary's red rose alcove fringed in blue
We absorb natures beauty all around

Now we look and see our Fiacre is missing
The verdant saint of healing herbs
Our garden patron will have a place anew
Here with emerald foliage all around

St Francis blesses hummingbirds and butterflies again
Industrious teenage grands did lessen the heavy toil
To their pride and pleasure the garden they rekindled
Bad weather, you are exiled, never again to spoil.

Ernest D. Cronin

Sarah Cynthia Sylvia Stout

Sarah Cynthia Sylvia Stout
Would not take the garbage out!
She'd scour the pots and scrub the pans,
Candy the yams and spice the hams,
And though her daddy would scream and shout,
She simply would not take the garbage out.
And so, it piled up to the ceilings:
Coffee grounds, potato peelings,
Brown bananas, rotten peas,
Chunks of sour cottage cheese.
It filled the can, it covered the floor,
Cracked the window and blocked the door
With bacon rinds and chicken bones,
Drippy ends of ice cream cones,
Prune pits, peach pits, orange peel,
Gloopy glumps of cold oatmeal,
Pizza crust and withered greens
Soggy beans and tangerines,
Crust of black burned buttered toast,
Gristly bits of beefy roasts...
The garbage rolled on down the hall,
It raised the roof, it broke the wall...
Greasy napkins, cookie crumbs,
Globs of gooey bubble gum,
Cellophane from green baloney,
Rubbery blubbery macaroni,
Peanut butter, caked and dry,
Curdled milk and crusts of pie,
Moldy melons, dried-up mustard,
Eggshells mixed with lemon custard,
Cold French fries and rancid meat,
Yellow lumps of Cream of Wheat.

At last, the garbage reached so high
That it finally touched the sky.
And all the neighbors moved away,
And none of her friends would come to play.
And finally, Sarah Cynthia Stout said,
"OK, I'll take the garbage out!"
But then, of course, it was too late...
The garbage reached across the state,
From New York to the Golden Gate,
And there, in the garbage she did hate,
Poor Sarah met an awful fate,
That I cannot right now relate
Because the hour is much too late.
But children, remember Sarah Stout
And always take the garbage out!

Shel Silverstein

Little Edgar Smith

Little Edgar Smith was ever so fat, you see.
But he was content with what he wanted to be.
He saw a sumo wrestler conquer all with glee.
Corpulence he trusted, would win the day foreseen.

He proudly joined his college scholastic wrestling team.
But he perceived correctly, his teammates were steamed
As his humongous frame mocked their bodies lean.
Still, he bested all their rivals to cheerfully please the team.

When he tried to court fulsome Lucinda Mc Bee
He discovered her cold shoulder stung like a bee.
But his fame was ascendant; Japan called him supreme.
So, Lucinda snared little Edgar and, with courtship, did sing

Edgar boasts of five little Smiths he sired.
Lucinda smiles and sighs, "Maybe I should retire."
Fate will take them where it will, no doubt.
They are linked together and happiness they shout.

Ernest D. Cronin

The Destruction of Sennacherib

The Assyrian came down like the wolf on the fold,
And his cohorts were gleaming in purple and gold;
And the sheen of their spears was like stars on the sea,
When the blue wave rolls nightly on deep Galilee.

Like the leaves of the forest when Summer is green,
That host with their banners at sunset were seen:
Like the leaves of the forest when Autumn hath blown,
That host on the morrow lay withered and strown.

For the Angel of Death spread his wings on the blast,
And breathed in the face of the foe as he passed;
And the eyes of the sleepers waxed deadly and chill,
And their hearts but once heaved, and forever grew still!

And there lay the steed with his nostril all wide,
But through it there rolled not the breath of his pride;
And the foam of his gasping lay white on the turf,
And cold as the spray of the rock-beating surf.

And there lay the rider distorted and pale,
With the dew on his brow, and the rust on his mail:
And the tents were all silent, the banners alone,
The lances unlifted, the trumpet unblown.

And the widows of Ashur are loud in their wail,
And the idols are broke in the temple of Baal;
And the might of the Gentile, unsmote by the sword,
Hath melted like snow in the glance of the Lord!

Lord Byron "George Gordon"

If—

If you can keep your head when all about you
　Are losing theirs and blaming it on you,
If you can trust yourself when all men doubt you,
　But make allowance for their doubting too;
If you can wait and not be tired by waiting,
　Or being lied about, don't deal in lies,
Or being hated, don't give way to hating,
　And yet don't look too good, nor talk too wise:

If you can dream—and not make dreams your master;
　If you can think—and not make thoughts your aim;
If you can meet with Triumph and Disaster
　And treat those two impostors just the same;
If you can bear to hear the truth you've spoken
　Twisted by knaves to make a trap for fools,
Or watch the things you gave your life to, broken,
　And stoop and build 'em up with worn-out tools:

If you can make one heap of all your winnings
　And risk it on one turn of pitch-and-toss,
And lose, and start again at your beginnings
　And never breathe a word about your loss;
If you can force your heart and nerve and sinew
　To serve your turn long after they are gone,
And so hold on when there is nothing in you
　Except the Will which says to them: 'Hold on!'

If you can talk with crowds and keep your virtue,
　Or walk with Kings—nor lose the common touch,
If neither foes nor loving friends can hurt you,
　If all men count with you, but none too much;
If you can fill the unforgiving minute

With sixty seconds' worth of distance run,
Yours is the Earth and everything that's in it,
And—which is more—you'll be a Man, my son!

Rudyard Kipling

Marcus Aurelius One-liners

"Our life is what our thoughts make it."

"If it is not right do not do it; if it is not true do not say it."

"Little is needed to make a happy life; it is all within yourself in your way of thinking."

"The first rule is to keep an untroubled spirit, and the second is to look things in the face and know them for what they are."

"Waste no more time arguing about what a good man should be. Be one."

Marcus Aurelius

Mother Teresa #1

"Not all of us can do great things. But we can do small things with great love."

"Kind words can be short and easy to speak, but their echoes are truly endless."

"If you can't feed a hundred people, then feed just one."

"Yesterday is gone. Tomorrow has not yet come. We have only today. Let us begin."

"We shall never know all the good that a simple smile can do." "Love cannot remain by itself – it has no meaning. Love has to be put into action, and that action is service."

"It is a poverty to decide that a child must die so that you may live as you wish."

Mother Teresa #2

"The most terrible poverty is loneliness, and the feeling of being unloved."

"I alone cannot change the world, but I can cast a stone across the waters to create many ripples."

"God doesn't require us to succeed, He only requires that you try."

"If we have no peace, it is because we have forgotten that we belong to each other."

"It's not how much we give, but how much love we put into giving."

"Joy is a net of love in which you can catch souls."

Mother Teresa #3

"Never travel faster than your guardian angel can fly."

"Let us always meet each other with a smile, for the smile is the beginning of love."

"If you are humble, nothing will touch you, neither praise nor disgrace, because you know what you are."

"Do not wait for leaders; do it alone, person to person."

"We must not be surprised when we hear of murders, killings, of wars, or of hatred… The greatest destroyer of peace is abortion, because if a mother can kill her own child, what is left for me to kill you and you to kill me? There is nothing between."

"I do not pray for success; I ask for faithfulness."

"Any country that accepts abortion is not teaching its people to love but to use violence to get what they want."

Mother Teresa #4

"Life is a song, sing it. Life is a struggle, accept it."

"Some people come in our lives as blessings. Some come in your life as lessons."

"How can there be too many children? That is like saying there are too many flowers."

"If you find happiness, people may be jealous. Be happy anyway."

"What you spend years building may be destroyed overnight; build it anyway."

"Give the world the best you have, and it may never be enough; give the world the best you've got anyway."

"One filled with the joy preaches without preaching."

"I know God will not give me anything I can't handle. I just wish that he didn't trust me so much."

The LORD is My Shepherd

The LORD is my shepherd; I shall not want.

He maketh me to lie down in green pastures: he leadeth me beside the still waters.

He restoreth my soul: he leadeth me in the paths of righteousness for his name's sake.

Yea, though I walk through the valley of the shadow Of death, I will fear no evil: for thou art with me; thy rod and thy staff they comfort me.

Thou preparest a table before me in the presence of mine enemies: thou anointest my head with oil; my cup runneth over.

Surely goodness and mercy shall follow me all the days of my life: and I will dwell in the house of the LORD forever.

Holy Bible, Psalm 23, KJV

The Words of the Preacher

The words of the Preacher, the son of David,
king in Jerusalem.

Vanity of vanities, saith the Preacher, vanity of vanities;
all is vanity.

What profit hath a man of all his labour which he taketh under the
sun?

Holy Bible, Ecclesiastes 1:1-3

About Dr. Cronin

Dr. Cronin published his memoir, *The Healing Mission of Plastic Surgery, One Surgeons Story* in 2020. It received the following favorable reviews.
https://bit.ly/Healing-Mission

"Over three decades ago, I met a seemingly simple, quiet, unassuming individual. I quickly appreciated how privileged I was to be in the presence of greatness. In Dr. Ernest Cronin's Healing Mission of Plastic Surgery, a skilled, compassionate sagacious surgeon, sage, philosopher, and friend provides an honest glimpse into the life of a living legend.
-- **Gary Branfman**, MD, FACS, Plastic Surgeon

"Enlightening, memorable, professional, this amazing Book has it all. Do read this unusual personal story of the healing journey of a life spent as a plastic surgeon."
-- **Donna R. Fox**, PhD, Speech Pathologist, Fellow ASLHA and Professor Emeritus, University of Houston

"It is a great honor and a pleasure for me to recommend this fascinating book highly. It chronologically summarizes Dr. Ernest Cronin's professional career in the field of Plastic and Reconstructive Surgery, witnessing and participating in significant advances in the specialty throughout four decades. Dr. Ernest Cronin is a generous humanitarian who has improved countless patients' lives and mentored many plastic surgeons, including me."
-- **Alfonso Barrera**, MD, FACS, Clinical Assistant Professor Baylor College of

Medicine and author of *Hair Transplantation*

"Like a great conductor, Dr. Ernest Cronin Masterfully orchestrated the sequence and tempo of every surgery. Every action served a purpose---he wasted no motion. His technical savvy, coupled with his kindness and compassion, made him the best surgeon with whom I ever worked."
-- **Henry Mentz**, MD, FACS Aesthetic Center for Plastic Surgery. Awarded - Best Plastic Surgeon of the Year for US 2016-20 by Medical Livewire, A.I., Global 100, M&A, Leading Advisor, The Global Venture

"One word for this book - SENSATIONAL - a gem! - great experience, excellent surgical results, clear explanations, good artwork, and all presented in a simple conversational way. I feel as if every resident should read it. The book presents a huge experience in Plastic surgery as a real "healing mission."
-- **Thomas Biggs**, MD, FACS Clinical Professor Plastic Surgery Baylor College of Medicine, ICON of the American Association of Plastic Surgeons, Former Presidents of the International Society of Aesthetic Plastic Surgery

"Dr. Cronin is one of the finest plastic surgeons in the country."
-- **Marvin Zindler**, former KPRC TV Personality, Houston, March 1st, 2000

"Dr. Ernest Cronin, a true legend in International Plastic Surgery, has graced our literature with... his experiences, successes, and failures... a wonderful

treatise... beautifully illustrated!"
-- **Donald H. Parks**, BA, MD, FRCS, FACS,
Professor of Surgery, McGovern Medical
School, University of Texas Health Science
Center Houston, Chief, Division of Plastic Surgery (Retired)

www.ingramcontent.com/pod-product-compliance
Lightning Source LLC
Chambersburg PA
CBHW071858070526
44583CB00016B/1750